The EVERYTHING KIDS' Picture Puzzles Book

Hidden pictures, matching games, pattern puzzles, and more!

Beth L. Blair and Jennifer A. Ericsson

Adams Media

New York   London   Toronto   Sydney   New Delhi

Adams Media
An Imprint of Simon & Schuster, Inc.
57 Littlefield Street
Avon, Massachusetts 02322

For information about special discounts for bulk purchases, please contact Simon & Schuster Special Sales at 1-866-506-1949 or business@simonandschuster.com.

The Simon & Schuster Speakers Bureau can bring authors to your live event. For more information or to book an event contact the Simon & Schuster Speakers Bureau at 1-866-248-3049 or visit our website at www.simonspeakers.com.

Interior illustrations by Kurt Dolber.
Puzzles by Beth L. Blair.

Manufactured in the United States of America

Printed by LSC Communications, Harrisonburg, VA, U.S.A.

10 9 8 7 6 5 4 3 2 1
November 2013

ISBN 978-1-4405-7067-4

Contains material adapted and abridged from: *The Everything® Kids' Animal Puzzle and Activity Book* by Beth L. Blair and Jennifer A. Ericsson, copyright © 2005 by Simon & Schuster, Inc., ISBN 10: 1-59337-305-8, ISBN 13: 978-1-59337-305-4; *The Everything® Kids' Basketball Book* by Bob Schaller with Coach Dave Harnish, copyright © 2009 by Simon & Schuster, Inc., ISBN 10: 1-60550-165-4, ISBN 13: 978-1-60550-165-9; *The Everything® Kids' Christmas Puzzle and Activity Book* by Beth L. Blair and Jennifer A. Ericsson, copyright © 2003 by Simon & Schuster, Inc., ISBN 10: 1-58062-965-2, ISBN 13: 978-1-58062-965-2; *The Everything® Kids' Crazy Puzzles Book* by Beth L. Blair and Jennifer A. Ericsson, copyright © 2005 by Simon & Schuster, Inc., ISBN 10: 1-59337-361-9, ISBN 13: 978-1-59337-361-0; *The Everything® Kids' Football Book, 3rd Edition* by Greg Jacobs, copyright © 2012, 2010, 2008 by Simon & Schuster, Inc., ISBN 10: 1-4405-4009-8, ISBN 13: 978-1-4405-4009-7; *The Everything® Kids' Halloween Puzzle and Activity Book* by Beth L. Blair and Jennifer A. Ericsson, copyright © 2003 by Simon & Schuster, Inc., ISBN 10: 1-58062-959-8, ISBN 13: 978-1-58062-959-1; *The Everything® Kids' Hanukkah Puzzle and Activity Book* by Beth L. Blair and Jennifer A. Ericsson with Rabbi Hyim Shafner, copyright © 2008 by Simon & Schuster, Inc., ISBN 10: 1-59869-788-9, ISBN 13: 978-1-59869-788-9; *The Everything® Kids' Hidden Pictures Book* by Beth L. Blair, copyright © 2004 by Simon & Schuster, Inc., ISBN 10: 1-59337-128-9, ISBN 13: 978-1-59337-128-4; *The Everything® Kids' More Hidden Pictures Book* by Beth L. Blair, copyright © 2010 by Simon & Schuster, Inc., ISBN 10: 1-4405-0614-0, ISBN 13: 978-1-4405-0614-7; *The Everything® Kids' Puzzle Book* by Jennifer A. Ericsson and Beth L. Blair, copyright © 2000 by Simon & Schuster, Inc., ISBN 10: 1-58062-687-3, ISBN 13: 978-1-58062-687-4; and *The Everything® Kids' Soccer Book, 2nd Edition* by Deborah W. Crisfield, copyright © 2009, 2002 by Simon & Schuster, Inc., ISBN 10: 1-60550-162-X, ISBN 13: 978-1-60550-162-8.

Many of the designations used by manufacturers and sellers to distinguish their products are claimed as trademarks. Where those designations appear in this book and Simon & Schuster, Inc., was aware of a trademark claim, the designations have been printed with initial capital letters.

Contents

CHAPTER 1

Playtime with Friends

PLEASE RECYCLE

Pass It On

Parker tried to pass this funny joke to Toshi during math class. When he got caught, Parker ripped up the note. Can you piece it back together so you can have a good laugh, too? Write the fixed-up joke on the blank piece of paper.

yes at pick them

should if a rolls

roll back!

up and them

What you do teacher

his e you?

How Many Marbles?

Sandy, Peter, and Flo are playing marbles. To find out how many marbles each child has, add the numbers that make a straight line through the circle from where each player shoots.

Jumble of Jacks

Find your way from the first jack to the ball.

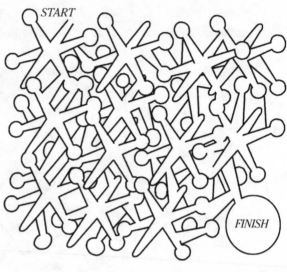

START

FINISH

Two of a Kind

You are holding a handful of Kings, and two of them are exactly the same. Which two are they?

Go Fish

Can you tell who is winning this round of Go Fish? While you figure that out, see if you can find the 9 fish hiding in this picture.

Sleepover

These two friends are fast asleep. Can you find everything that one of the girls brought for her sleepover? Look for a **backpack**, **toothbrush**, **tube of toothpaste**, **nightgown**, **book**, **pair of socks**, and **hairbrush**.

Our Club

The two friends on the page to the left are hiding up in their tree house. Can you find the following 16 items that are hiding in the picture with them? Look for a **butterfly**, **carrot**, **paintbrush**, **snail**, **belt**, **horn**, **baseball cap**, **pair of scissors**, **squirrel**, **paper clip**, **capital letter E**, **fork**, **elephant face**, **slice of pizza**, **clothes hanger**, and **heart**.

Crazy Hats

These two friends bought the same crazy hats . . . or did they? See if you can find five hidden items. Some are in one hat, and some are in the other! You are looking for a **referee's whistle**, **paper clip**, **heart**, **wristwatch**, **banana**, and **fried egg**.
EXTRA FUN: Now try to find five more differences between the two hats!

Driveway Art

Tony has an under-the-sea theme going down the driveway.
He's drawing a whale right now, but can you also find
the **fish**, **eel**, **crab**, **starfish**, **scallop shell**, **seahorse**,
and **jellyfish** that are hidden on this page?

Choo Choo

Emma and Ryan like to take out the trains and cars and spread out all over the living room floor! Can you find these 10 items hiding on the facing page with all the toys? You are looking for a **chicken**, **teacup**, **2 cat faces**, **leaf**, **comb**, **letter X**, **smiley face**, **paper clip**, and **slice of pizza**.

Goal!

Soccer can be a mad scramble to run after the ball and try to score a point. How many times can you find the complete word **G-O-A-L** hiding among the flying feet?

In the Shadows

Mieko and Harry are making shadow puppets on the wall. Can you find the pattern that exactly matches the picture to the right?

CHAPTER 2

The World of Animals

Peacock

Can you find 17 things in this pretty peacock that start with the letter P?

Bird Watching

Sometimes if you're very quiet, you can see where a mother bird has hidden her nest. Try to find the following items that are hiding in the trees with her! Look for a **bunny**, **sock**, **heart**, **whale**, **kite**, **crown**, **pair of dice**, **three jacks**, **mitten**, **teapot**, **star**, and **pair of scissors**.

Leaping Lizards

Desert lizards can have very different shapes: geckos are soft and squashy; whiptails have long, thin tails; skinks are little and skinny; horned lizards are covered with spikes. Can you tell which two lizards do not appear on both sides of the page?

Pig Pen

On a hot day, a poor pig can't sweat to cool off like you do. Pigs have no sweat glands! That's why pigs love to roll in nice, squishy mud. It not only cools them off, but helps protect their tender skin from the sun. Can you find the ten differences between these two pig pens?

Trick Question 1

Can you spell PIG using nine letters? Sure you can! Use a simple number substitution (A=1, B=2, C=3 . . .) to see how it is done.

Trick Question 2

All of Farmer Jane's pigs are brown except one, and all of her pigs are pink except one. How many brown and pink pigs does Farmer Jane have?

Rescue Dogs

Search and Rescue dogs are trained to find people who are lost in all kids of places. This dog is practicing in a forest. Can you find the 9 hidden people before Jasper the dog does?

RESCUE

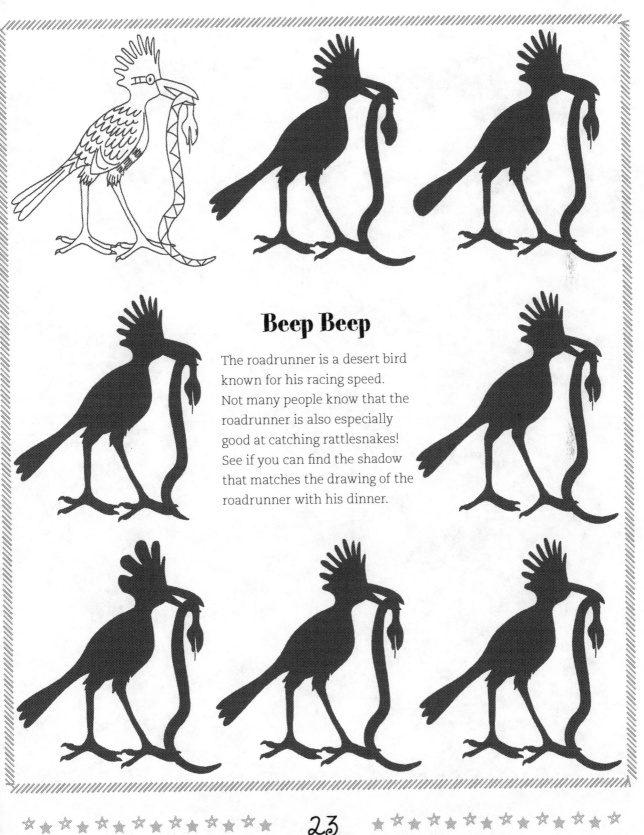

Beep Beep

The roadrunner is a desert bird known for his racing speed. Not many people know that the roadrunner is also especially good at catching rattlesnakes! See if you can find the shadow that matches the drawing of the roadrunner with his dinner.

Great Goldfish

A fancy goldfish makes a wonderful pet that can live for many years. Check this fish tank carefully to make sure there is nothing in there that can harm Ruby the goldfish!

Panda?

While they may look cuddly, giant pandas would rather be left alone to sleep, eat bamboo, and play. See if you can find the very, very shy panda hiding on the facing page.

What Pet Did Annie Get?

Annie just came home with her new pet. Can you figure out what it is? Cross off the pets Annie didn't get as you read these statements. When you're finished, only one pet will be left!

Does not live underwater.

Does not have wings.

Does not have a shell.

Does not have fur.

Does not have eight legs.

Does not have spots.

Pretty Poisonous

Poison-dart frogs are very small, multicolored tree frogs. Their bright colors signal predators to "stay away!" Not only will the frog taste bad, but the poisonous skin will make any animal who eats them sick. Using the color key below, color in these beautiful, but dangerous, frogs.

R = red   O = orange
B = blue   Y = yellow
G = green   P = purple
                 K = black

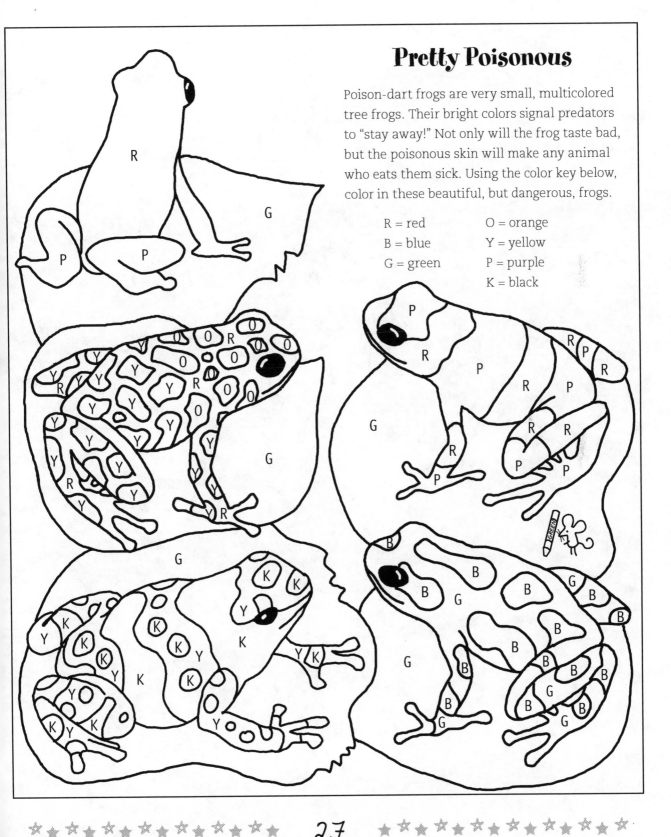

Best Friends

These two pals share everything, even their snacks! See if you can find 2 each of **chicken legs**, **fish**, **strips of bacon**, **slices of pizza**, and **dog bones**.

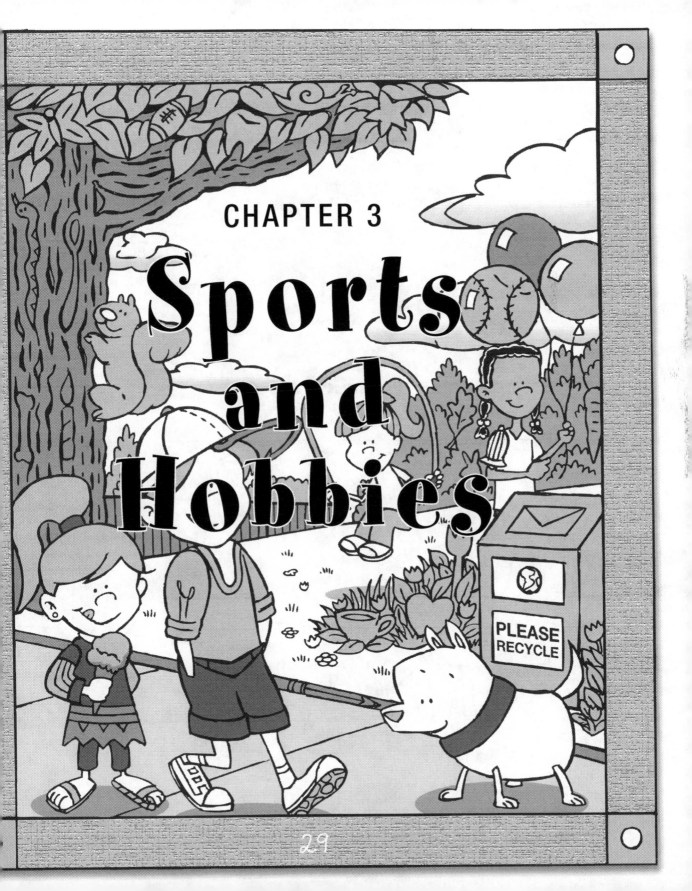

CHAPTER 3

Sports and Hobbies

In the Wild

Ryan's family packed in a hurry for their camping trip. Take a good look at the picture of their campsite, right. Can you see what fourteen items they brought by mistake?

Triangle Teaser

Color in each three-sided shape to find out where your dog sleeps when he goes camping with you.

Court Count

This game has gotten completely out of hand! There are 2 players on the court who don't belong. Can you spot them?

The Fingers of One Hand
On a 10-player team, only 5 players are allowed on the court at any one time.

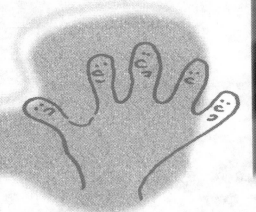

ZAP!

These two brothers are trying to see who can get the most points playing this computer game. You can play, too! See how many times you can find the word Z-A-P hiding in the border of this page. Multiply the number of ZAPs by 10 to get your score. The brothers' top score so far is 90. Did you beat them?

Sticky Stamps

Artie dropped his stamp collection and needs help resorting them!
See if you can answer the following questions:

1. Are there more patriotic stamps or stamps with birds?
2. What kind of creature is featured on the most stamps?
3. There are four stamps that are almost identical. What object is on each one?
4. What stamp has the most postage?

Downhill Race

These kids want to see who can make it down the hill first. They don't know that there are 17 hidden items racing down the hill with them! See if you can find the **snake**, **star**, **beaver**, **question mark**, **angel**, **sock**, **kite**, **umbrella**, **pair of dice**, **fish hook**, **comb**, **capital letter W**, **caterpillar**, **light bulb**, **camera**, and **ice cream cone**.

Fractured Football

The linebacker hit this football so hard it was broken in half! Which two pieces will fit together to make one complete ball?

Uniform Uniforms

Oops—goalies are supposed to wear shirts that are different from the rest of the team. These goalies look too much the same! Cross out the three pairs of goalies who are wearing exactly the same shirts. Circle the one goalie who has a shirt that is different from everyone else's. This goalie will get to play today!

College Copies

There are a lot of college basketball players with very similar skills. Sometimes they're so close it's hard to tell them apart! Can you see the 10 differences here?

Why did the chicken cross the basketball court?
He heard the referee calling fowls!

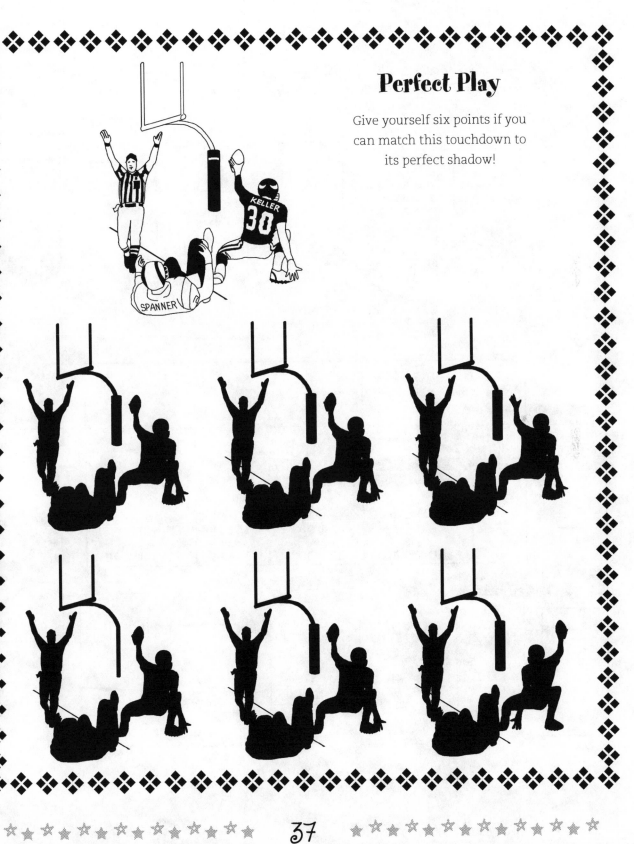

Perfect Play

Give yourself six points if you can match this touchdown to its perfect shadow!

Build a Model

To construct the model airplane, write the correct part number for each piece on the lines provided. The number shows where each piece belongs in the puzzle grid. We've given you a small picture of the completed airplane to guide you. Caution: Some of the pieces may be upside-down!

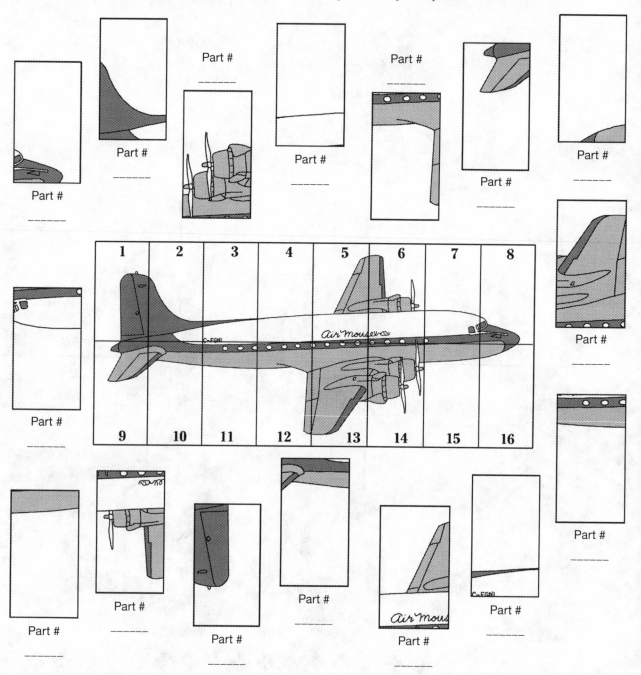

Part #
_____

Part #
_____

Part #
_____

Part #
_____

Part #
_____

Part #
_____

Part #
_____

Part #
_____

Part #
_____

Part #
_____

Part #
_____

Part #
_____

Part #
_____

Part #
_____

Part #
_____

Part #
_____

1	2	3	4	5	6	7	8
9	10	11	12	13	14	15	16

X-treme Sports
Decipher the picture puzzles to find the names of four wild-and-crazy sports!

On Your Mark!
Find the 14 reasons why these kids would be crazy to go swimming!

Goofy Golf

Giorgio loves to play goofy golf. You will, too!
Here are the rules:

* You must go to every hole.
* Count the dots you hit along each path.
  Each dot is worth 5 points.
* Add the value of the hole.
* You get a 20-point bonus on any hole with
  an even-numbered score.

Snake

Windmill

Penguin

Flamingo

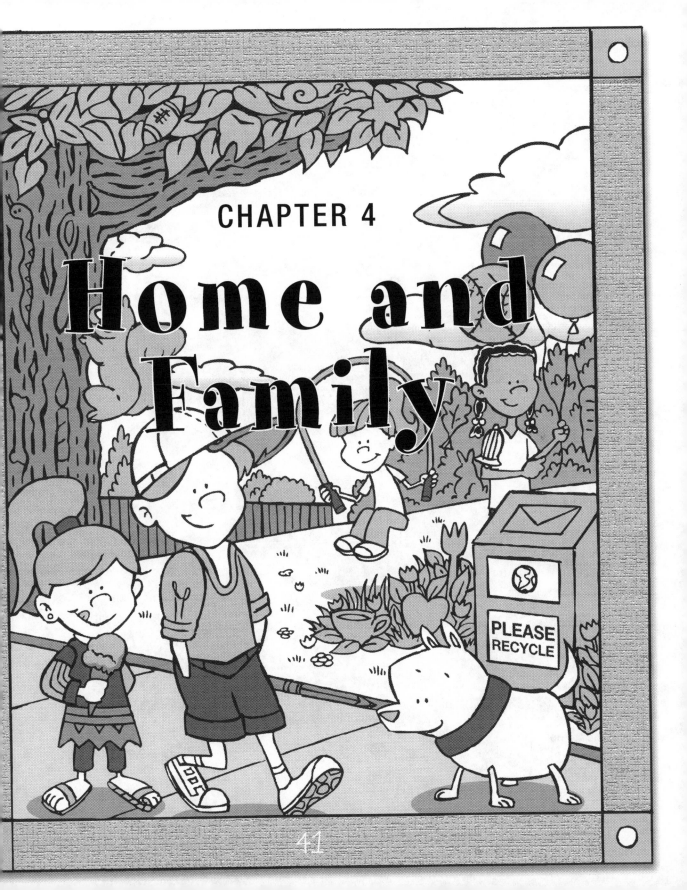

CHAPTER 4

Home and Family

Name Game

The people in this family have normal names, but they sure have a strange way of acting out what they are! Match each name in the list to the correct family member.

Alexis   José   Angelina   Matt   Noah
Art   Carol   Abigail   Mark   Isaac

Who's in the Family?

Carefully study this picture. Use the hidden clues to figure out how many family members use this kitchen. Pets count, too!

Sorting Laundry

The Murphy boys are doing chores today. Help them answer the following questions:

* Do all the socks match into pairs?
* Which pair of socks is different from all the others?
* Are there more shorts or T-shirts?
* Are the shirts correctly numbered from 1 to 8?

Good Night!

Uncle Chris read Andrew a scary story just before bedtime. Now Andrew sees monsters everywhere! Can you find the seven monsters, and the three words "MONSTER" in his room?

What's Weird?

Can you find the 16 things that are not quite normal in this house?

Twice the Fun

Krystal and Kayla think it's great that there is a Twins Festival celebrated each August in Twinsburg, Ohio!

Most days the girls wear the exact same dress and hairstyle, but today there are 6 differences. Can you find them?

Yard Work

Help the kids find these objects as they rake leaves: **ice cream cone, kite, racecar, mitten, fish head, flagpole, playing card, capital H, umbrella, tennis racket, tepee, star, mouse, tic-tac-toe board.**

Family Reunion

Find the word "**HUGS**" 11 times in this happy family reunion. See if you can also find the **snake**, **snowman**, **kite**, **teapot**, **snail**, **umbrella**, **lightning bolt**, and **head of a bunny**.

Stephanie's Sleepover

Stephanie had a gigantic sleepover party—there were 15 kids all together! The girls were being silly and arranged their sleeping bags to look like the following impossible math equation:

However, four of the guests had to go home early. After they left, Stephanie noticed that the math equation now worked! Can you figure out which four bags were taken away? Color in the remaining bags to see the numbers clearly.

Nice Neighbors

Nina, Lauren, Blair, and Dylan all live in the same neighborhood. Using the clues, can you decide in which house each child lives?

* Nina lives on Pine Street.
* Dylan lives diagonally across the street from Blair.
* Lauren lives down the street from Nina, but on the opposite side.
* Blair lives across the street from Nina.
* Lauren and Dylan live in the same block, but not on the same street.
* Blair does not live on Pine Street.
* Nina must cross Pine Street to visit Blair or Dylan.

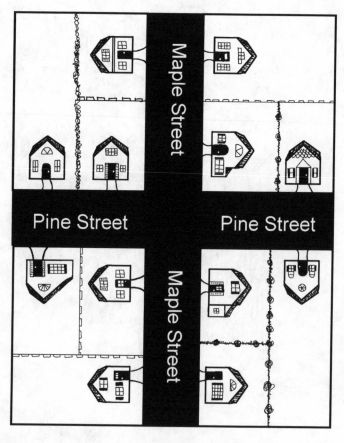

Family Portrait

Can you find the 12 differences between the two pictures of this family?

Dish Duty

Kiki and Matt are cleaning up after dinner.

Can you help them find 7 teacups, 3 glasses, 3 forks, and 1 knife?

CHAPTER 5

The Big Blue Sea

At the Shore

Not all ocean animals live in the deep sea. Many of them can be found at the shore, where the land meets the water. How many of each animal can you find in this picture?

HINT: Some animals are where you might expect to find them, and some are hiding in unexpected places.

crab

scallop

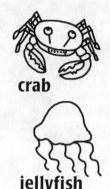

jellyfish

starfish

Sharks, Etc.

How many sharks can you find swimming in this ocean? Count shark noses or shark tails as 1 whole shark!

Extra Fun: How many jellyfish are hiding in with the sharks? What 1 item totally doesn't belong in this picture?

Walrus

On summer days off the coast of Alaska, you can sometimes see thousands of male walruses basking in the sun. Thousands of walruses mean twice that number of long white tusks. What could these guys really use? A good toothbrush! See if you can find 1.

Where Are We?

Color in all the penguins that have X, Y, or Z on them.
Read the remaining letters from left to right, top to bottom to get the answer to this riddle:
What do you call a colony of penguins living in the Arctic?

EXTRA FUN: What's the difference between the Arctic and Antarctica?
Check out the great maps and fascinating fun facts at this website: *www.worldatlas.com*.

A Day at the Beach

It's easy to get lost in a crowd. Can you spy where each of these small
parts is located in the big picture?
Hint: The small parts might be turned sideways or upside-down!

1. 2. 3. 4. 5. 6.

Lights, Please!

Most sea creatures live in water that is warmed by the sun. But some live deep in the sea where it is cold and dark. Creatures who live down there must make their own light! Use a white gel pen to connect the dots from 1 to 99 and you will see a very strange deep-ocean fish.

EXTRA FUN: When you are done, use a pale green crayon to color the glowing lanterns that hang from his chin and forehead. This fish uses them to lure dinner out of the dark and close to his terrible teeth!

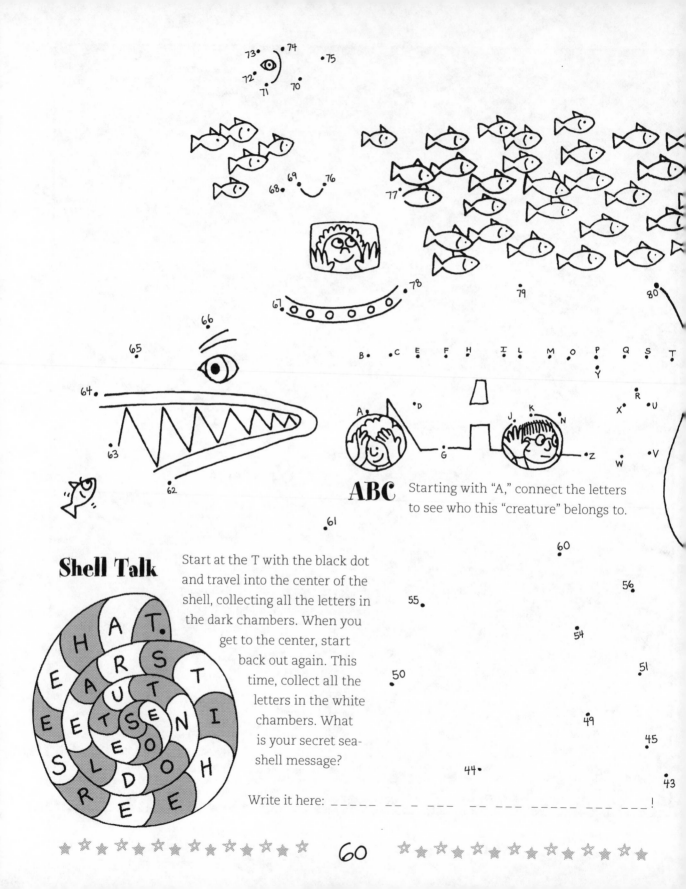

ABC Starting with "A," connect the letters to see who this "creature" belongs to.

Shell Talk

Start at the T with the black dot and travel into the center of the shell, collecting all the letters in the dark chambers. When you get to the center, start back out again. This time, collect all the letters in the white chambers. What is your secret sea-shell message?

Write it here: _ !

School of Fish

Fish traveling in groups called schools move so fast that they are hard to count! First, guess how many fish are in this school. Then, circle them in groups of five. Catching them this way makes counting easier.

Your Guess	Exact Number

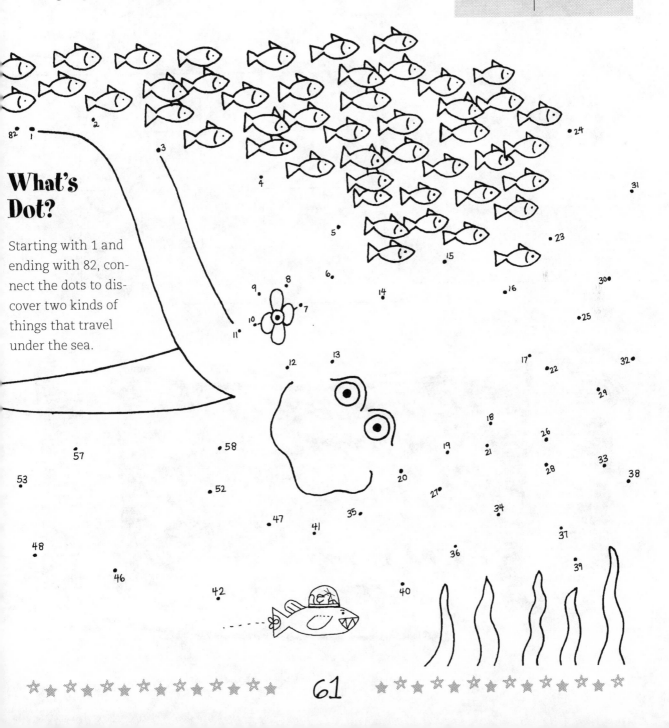

What's Dot?

Starting with 1 and ending with 82, connect the dots to discover two kinds of things that travel under the sea.

X Marks the Spot

Treasure could be buried at any of the X spots on this map. Using the compass and following the directions below, you should be able to find the right one.

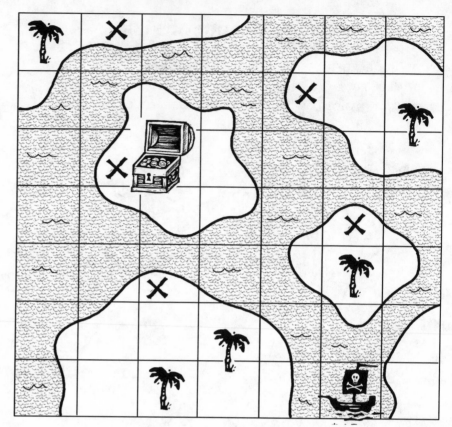

Start

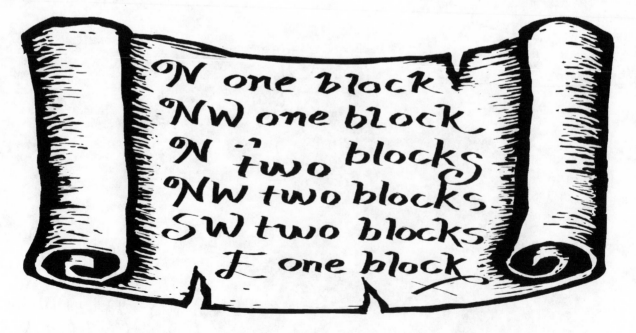

N one block
NW one block
N two blocks
NW two blocks
SW two blocks
E one block

Create a Fish

Some of these names of real fish might give you ideas of how to draw silly fish! Use the shapes provided to start your drawings. Color your fish when finished!

PARROTFISH
CLOWNFISH
TRUMPETFISH
PENCILFISH
FLAGTAIL
DOTTYBACK

1.

2.

3.

Crusty Fellow

Look closely at the plants in this picture. They will tell you the silly answer to this unlikely question:

Why wouldn't the lobster share his toys?

Nice Neigh-bor

What ocean animal has a snout like a trumpet, a pouch like a kangaroo, and a grasping tail like a monkey? Copy the pattern in each numbered square into the proper place in the grid, and you will find out!

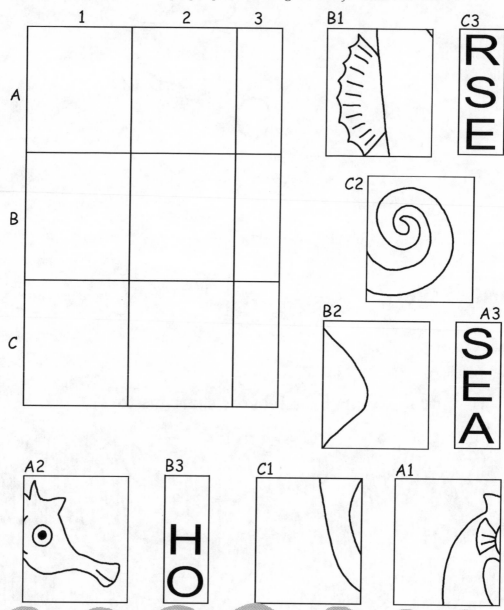

CHAPTER 6

Let's Eat!

PLEASE RECYCLE

Just One Bite-Please?

This big brother is being pretty patient, but the baby just doesn't want to eat lunch! Maybe he should take a break and see if he can find the 15 items hiding in the kitchen instead. There's a **musical note**, **ghost**, **comb**, **safety pin**, **car**, **flag**, **tube of toothpaste**, **capital letter L** and **capital letter M**, **paintbrush**, **thimble**, **fork**, **butterfly**, **cherry**, and **rubber duck**.

S·L·L·L·L·U·U·U·R·R·R·P!

Follow Rosie's super-long strand of pasta over and under from her slurping lips to the meatball at the bottom of the plate!

START

END

Sunday Dinner

Can you find 24 unusual additions to this funny family feast?

Super Salad

You might find all sorts of goodies hiding in a big bowl of salad—but you probably wouldn't want to see the following 21 items! Search among the lettuce leaves and see if you can find a **thimble, needle and thread, bug, bunny face, crown, bicycle, diamond, baseball cap, goldfish, spring, pair of eyeglasses, hatchet, bat, kite, two jacks, glove, clown's face, balloon, star,** and **Christmas tree!**

Grams is not happy to see that the "boys" are making faces with their food! She would be even less pleased to see the other 12 faces hiding in this picture! Can you find them? Look for a **bear**, **crocodile**, **frog**, **cat**, **owl**, **mouse**, **elephant**, **witch**, **puppy**, **man in the moon**, **bald man**, and **man with a long nose**.

Food Fun

Splash!

The ship's cook dropped dinner in the drink! Can you help him find his soggy supper? Look for a **piece of cheese on a cracker**, **orange slice**, **apple**, **bowl of spaghetti**, **bowl of salad**, **slice of bread**, **stick of butter**, **glass of water**, **ice-cream cone**, **salt shaker**, **knife**, **fork**, **spoon**, and **teacup**.

Scoops

Can you find the 19 items that you might not want to mix with ice cream? Look for a **snail**, **bird**, **mitten**, **umbrella**, **paperclip**, **cat's face**, **ghost**, **number 3**, **gingerbread man**, **fried egg**, **comb**, **pencil**, **earthworm**, **slice of bacon**, **horn**, **bubble pipe**, **snowman's face**, **pickle**, and **rocket ship**.

Hiding Hot Dogs

The family pets have found the perfect place to hide. Under the table it's quiet, dark, and people drop all kinds of good food down to you! See if you can find the other 11 items hiding in this picture. Look for a **bubble pipe**, **musical note**, **hot dog in a bun**, **goose**, **golf club**, **cane**, **diamond**, **domino**, **bat**, **bowling pin**, and **heart**.

Jesse is showing his friends how to make his favorite "bunny salad." In fact, bunnies like this salad so much, that bunches of them are hiding in the picture waiting for a taste! Can you find all 20 bunny faces?

EXTRA FUN: A bunny salad is simple to make. A canned pear half is the bunny body, cottage cheese is the tail, half a cherry is the nose, two long slices of banana are the ears, and the eyes are raisins.

Bunny Salad

Fill 'er Up!

The average person in America eats about 29 bowls of this tasty treat every year! Fill in all the shapes that have the letter C, R, U, N, C, or H to find the name of this popular snack.

Crazy Cookies

Can you find the two cookies that are decorated with the exact same face?

Sneaking Treats

The kids all love Gramma Ginny's cookies. They're trying to sneak a few while they're still hot from the oven! Can you find the 17 other items that have snuck into this picture, too? Look for a **book**, **gingerbread man**, **banana**, **teacup**, **sock**, **ladder**, **glove**, **three pieces of popcorn**, **coat hanger**, **candy cane**, **traffic light**, **umbrella**, **referee's whistle**, **domino**, and **turtle**?

CHAPTER 7

Travel Fun

Pack Your Bags!

These girls are getting ready for their vacation. Can you find at least eight shapes that are the same in both pictures? Be careful, the shape may be the same, but it might be used in a totally different way!

EXTRA FUN:
Take another look. What do you notice that is the opposite between these pictures?

Cross-Country Trip

Sonja is driving with her family from your home in Maine back to her house in California. On the way, she stops in eighteen states. At each stop she mails you a postcard with the state abbreviation on it. But the postcards do not arrive in order! See if you can plot Sonja's trip on the map below. Shade in each state as you put the postcards in order from Maine to California.

India

The weather in India is hot and humid. Women stay comfortable by wearing a thin fabric garment called a sari. Saris that are worn every day are made from plain fabric, but ones worn for special events are covered with beautiful patterns, embroidery, and even tiny mirrors!

These ladies are dressed up to go to the elephant festival. Can you find the **2 elephants** hiding in the pattern of their beautiful saris?

Peculiar Passport

This passport is strange—all of the country names are written in rebus form! Figure them out and write the real name underneath each country's stamp.

EXTRA STRANGE:
It would be impossible to get your passport stamped in one of these countries today. Do you know which one, and why?

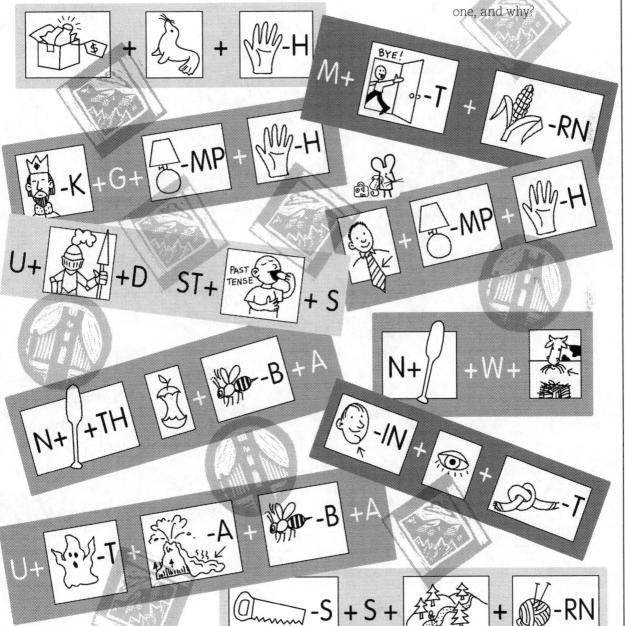

Mexico

Piñatas (peen-YAH-tahs) are colorful paper containers filled with candy and toys. They are enjoyed by Mexican children at birthday parties and festivals.

Piñatas are hung from a tree. Children wear blindfolds and swing at the piñata with a stick. When someone breaks it open, everyone scrambles to collect the treats!

Can you find the **11 pieces of candy corn** and the **7 lollipops**?

Road Trip

Dad is still trying to stuff the last few items into the back of the family van. Can you find 11 more hidden items that this family is taking along on their vacation? Look for a **paperclip**, **needle and thread**, **slice of bread**, **pear**, **hammer**, **pencil**, **adhesive bandage**, **light bulb**, **clock**, **phone receiver**, and **coffee mug**.

This tropical tourist spot holds a lot more than monkeys and toucans. Look for a **bow tie**, **mitten**, **ski hat**, **crown**, **teacup**, **kite**, **eyeglasses**, **banana**, **sock**, **scissors**, **bunny**, **spoon**, **heart**, **fork**, and **umbrella!**

Hidden Jungle

Wish You Were Here

Your friend is on vacation in North Carolina and sent you two of the same postcards. But are they really the same? See if you can find the following hidden items:

fishhook
mitten
needle
kite
letter E

EXTRA FUN:
After you find all of the hidden items, see if you can find five other ways in which these cards are different!

NORTH CAROLINA

NORTH COROLINA

France

The Eiffel Tower is one of the most famous symbols of France. It was built in 1889 for an international fair held in Paris.

Can you find the numbers 1-8-8-9 and the letters P-A-R-I-S hiding in this antique poster?

Check It Out!

This family is having a great vacation somewhere in the United States. By looking at the clues in the picture, can you figure out what state they are visiting?

EXTRA FUN: A famous scientist who worked with plants was born in this state. His name was George Washington Carver, and he figured out 325 different uses for the peanut! See if you can find the 18 peanuts hiding in this picture.

The Great Race

The Kripp family and the Krumm family are driving cross-country. Both families are starting in Maine, but they are following different routes.

The family with the lowest score wins!

Who will reach the West Coast first? To find out, follow these directions.

* Pick a different color for each family.
* Color the states through which each family will drive.
* Add up the number value for all states with one family's color, then the other.
* Sometimes one state will have two colors. That's OK.

KRIPP FAMILY	OH	ME	NH	VT
	IL	NY	PA	SD
	MT	IN	WI	MN
	OR	ND	ID	

KRUMM FAMILY	TX	PA	ME	MS
	CA	MA	NY	SC
	GA	AZ	NC	NH
	VA	AL	LA	NM

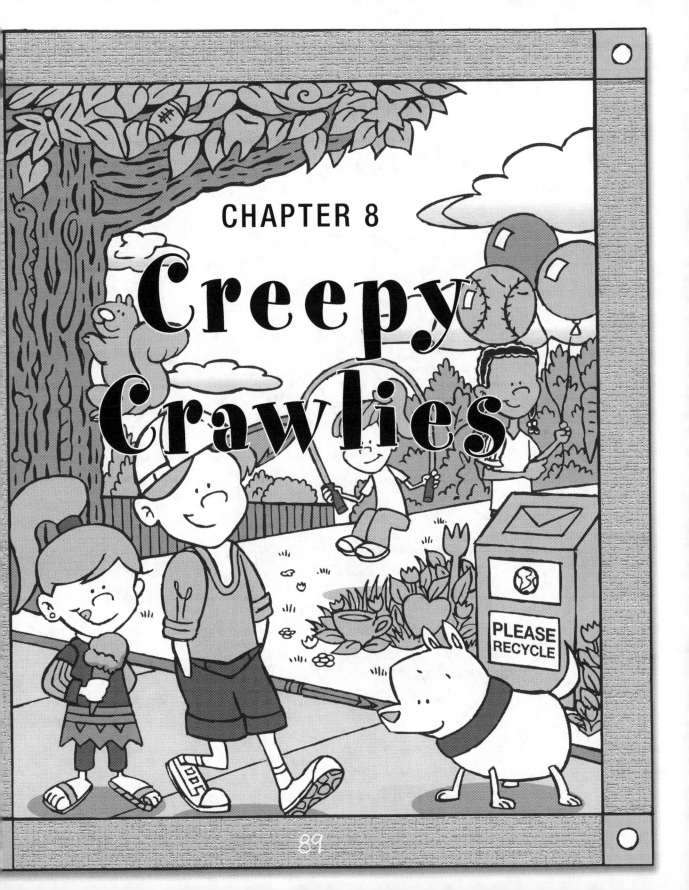

CHAPTER 8

Creepy Crawlies

Ants

Help the ants find their way across the blanket to the picnic. Stop at all the sweet treats, but go past the silverware.

Start

Creepy Crawlies

These kids found a lot of interesting things to study outside. Can you find the 15 items hiding in the picture, too? Look for a **whistle**, **umbrella**, **heart**, **bowling pin**, **snake**, **wishbone**, **toothbrush**, **banana**, **sword**, **pickle**, **spider**, **teacup**, **spoon**, **horn**, and **slice of bacon**.

Small Survivors

The desert is home to many small creatures who seem to survive there without much difficulty. There are five of these hidden in the word puzzle below. To find them, take one letter from each column moving from left to right. Cross them off as you go—each letter can only be used once. The first creature has been done for you.

```
S  O  I  T  L  T  S
C  P  E  U  E  T  S
B  E  C  D  S  E  T
L  E  R  C  K  R  E
T  R  X  M  I  E  S
```

1. _SPIDERS_
2. _____
3. _____
4. _____
5. _____

Small But Deadly

This desert hunter stays sheltered during the day. At night it comes out looking for prey, which it injects with deadly venom. Fill in the blocks as directed to see this small, but dangerous, creature. Would you like to meet one?

* Find box 1 and copy the pattern into square 1.
* Find box 2 and copy the pattern into square 2.
* Continue doing this until you have copied all the boxes into the grid.

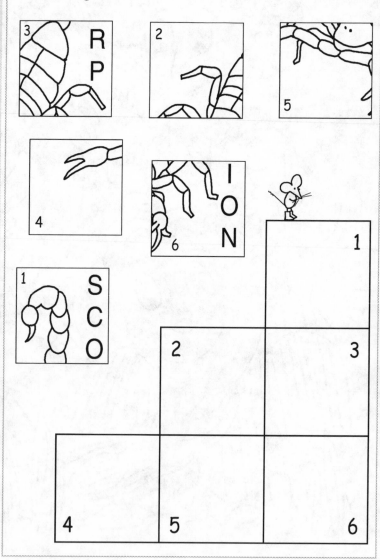

Summer Nights

The fireflies that these kids are trying to catch are easy to see because they are flashing brightly. It is not so easy to see the 17 items that are hidden in this dark yard. See if you can find a **broom**, **glove**, **gingerbread man**, **heart**, **umbrella**, **clothespin**, **wooden bucket**, **cane**, **ruler**, **pair of scissors**, **bow**, **toadstool**, **book**, **spoon**, **horseshoe**, **man's profile**, and **"The Big Dipper"**!

Why does everyone want spiders on their baseball team?

Pick up letters as you find the correct way through the web and around the bases from HIT to HOME RUN. Write them down in order and you will learn the answer to this riddle!

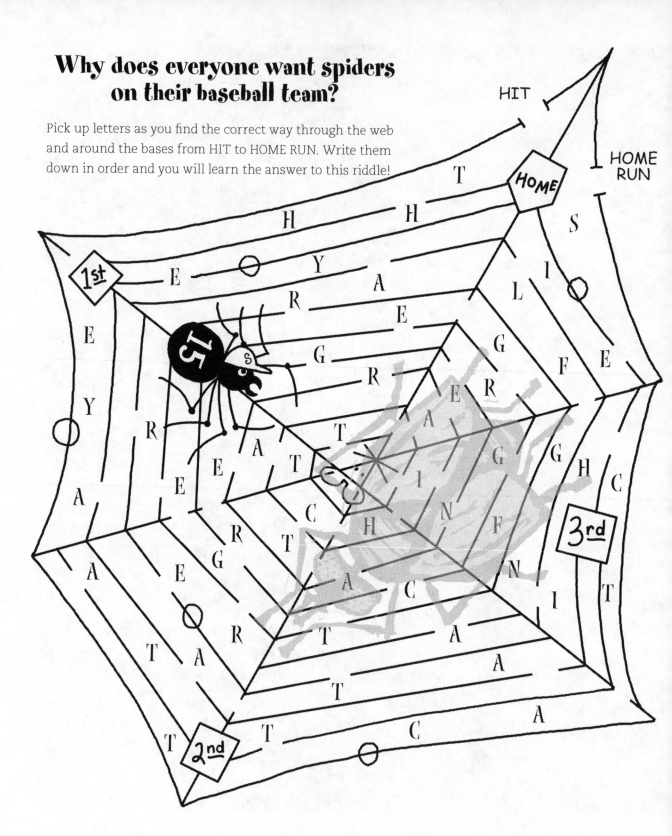

Sssssnakes

There are many desert snakes that have similar markings. If you are looking for a particular snake—especially one that is not poisonous—you had better be careful! Find the one snake below that has these four exact markings.

- **Light stripe down back**
- **White diamond on forehead**
- **Double diamond pattern on its body that looks like this** →
- **Rattle on end of tail**

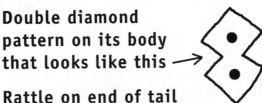

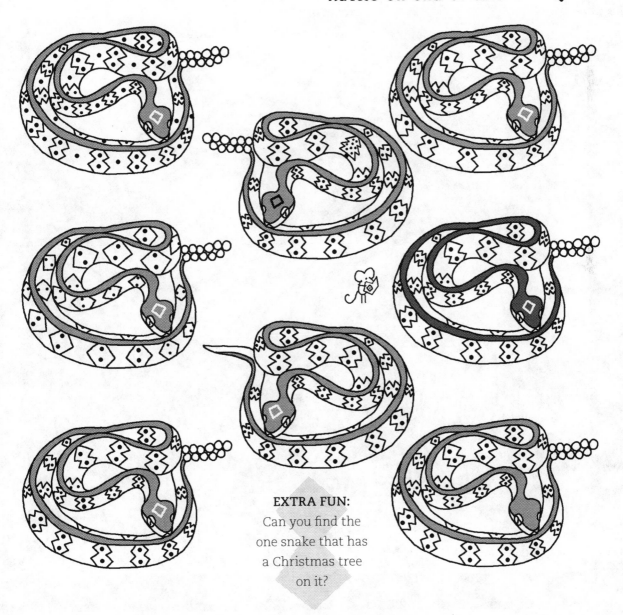

EXTRA FUN:
Can you find the one snake that has a Christmas tree on it?

Monarch Butterfly

In the fall, North American monarch butterflies fly to Mexico and California to spend the winter. By the time they return home the next spring, some butterflies will have traveled up to 3,000 miles! Find 7 letters that, when you put them in the correct order, will spell a word to describe this journey.

Extra Fun: Color the large white areas in the center of the wings bright orange. Color the dark edges of the wings and body black. Leave the small spots white.

Spider's Choice

Read the web from the center outward to see what spiders like to eat with their hamburgers.

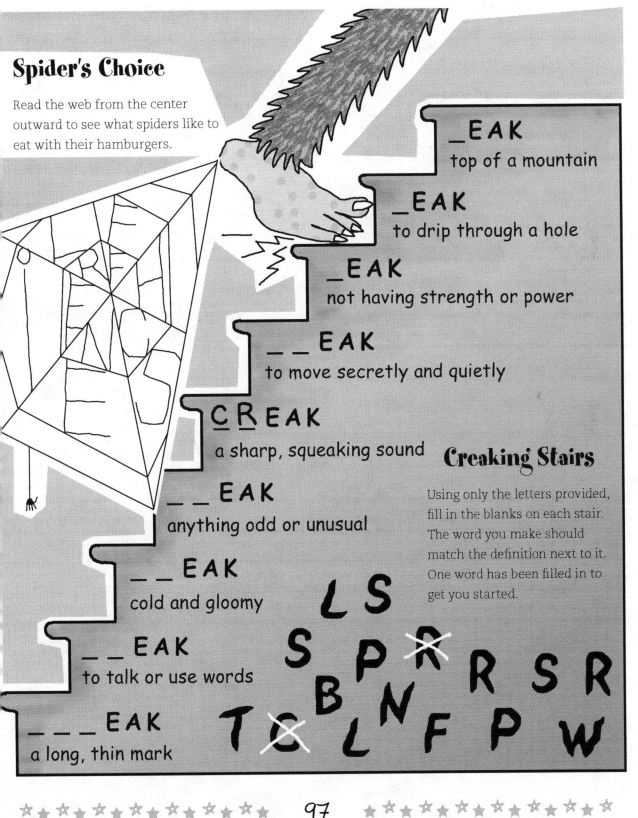

_ E A K
top of a mountain

_ E A K
to drip through a hole

_ E A K
not having strength or power

_ _ E A K
to move secretly and quietly

C R E A K
a sharp, squeaking sound

_ _ E A K
anything odd or unusual

_ _ E A K
cold and gloomy

_ _ E A K
to talk or use words

_ _ _ E A K
a long, thin mark

Creaking Stairs

Using only the letters provided, fill in the blanks on each stair. The word you make should match the definition next to it. One word has been filled in to get you started.

L S
S P R
R S R
B N
T C L F P W

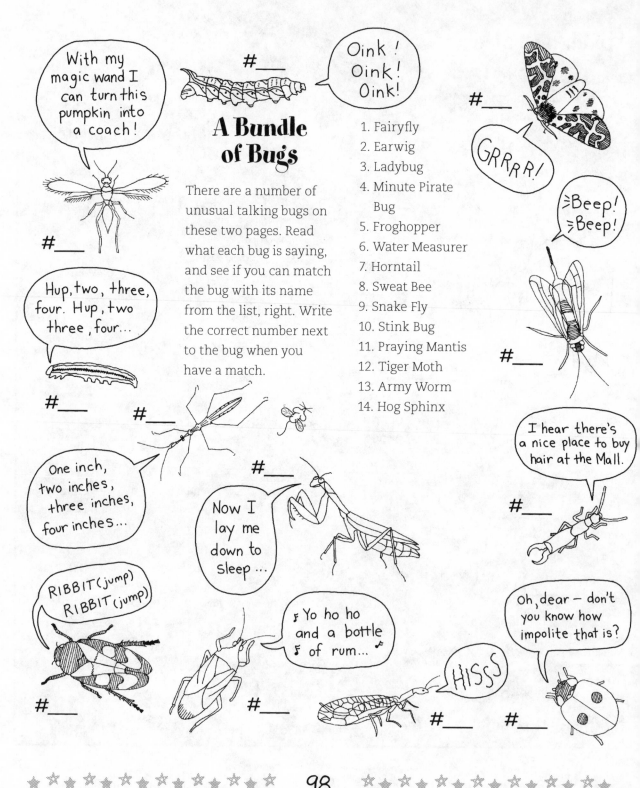

A Bundle of Bugs

There are a number of unusual talking bugs on these two pages. Read what each bug is saying, and see if you can match the bug with its name from the list, right. Write the correct number next to the bug when you have a match.

1. Fairyfly
2. Earwig
3. Ladybug
4. Minute Pirate Bug
5. Froghopper
6. Water Measurer
7. Horntail
8. Sweat Bee
9. Snake Fly
10. Stink Bug
11. Praying Mantis
12. Tiger Moth
13. Army Worm
14. Hog Sphinx

Pack Rat

Pack rats like to collect all sorts of things and pile them into big, messy nests. These critters particularly like objects that are shiny and bright! See if you can find what this rat has been taking from his neighbors. Look for a **thimble**, **whistle**, **button**, **ring**, **comb**, **pencil**, **key**, **eyeglasses**, **paper clip**, **coin**, **fishhook**, and **fork**.

Fun fact: If a pack rat lives in the desert, he might protect his nest with cactus spines!

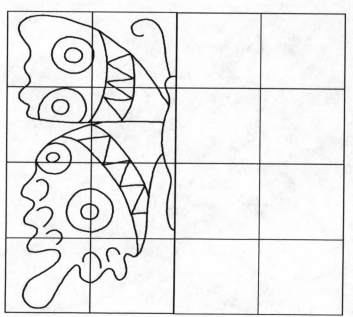

Breezy Butterflies

Believe it or not, there isn't much wind in a rainforest! Most rainforest plants need the animals and insects who live there to move their pollen and seeds around. Butterflies flit from flower to flower drinking nectar, and carry pollen from one plant to another as they go.

Draw the second half of this butterfly to match the half shown. Use the grid lines to guide you.

Batty for Fruit

Fruit bats use their keen sense of smell to find ripe rainforest fruit. By spitting out the seeds or dropping them as they fly through the forest, bats help new fruit trees to grow. Choose one of the dropped letters to add to each fruit. Then unscramble the letters and write the correct fruit names on the dotted lines.

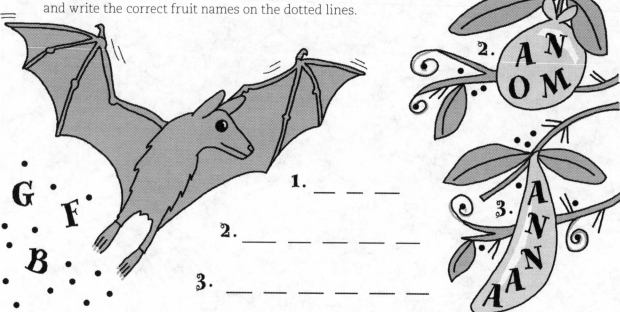

1. _ _ _ _ _ _

2. _ _ _ _ _ _

3. _ _ _ _ _ _

CHAPTER 9

Celebrations

Valentine's Day

Ryan is making a special card for his mom. Help him find **3 more hearts**, a **bottle of glue**, **tape**, and a **pencil**. Finally, find the six letters he will need to spell a familiar sentiment. Write the letters on the dotted lines!

_ _

_ _ _ _

And Many More . . .

Help great-grandpa celebrate his birthday by finding all the birthday candles.

EXTRA FUN: To find out how old gramps is today, take the number of candles, multiply by 10, and subtract 1.

Happy Half

Something is wrong with Hunter's instant camera. Only one half of each picture comes out! Can you help him by drawing in the rest of each party picture?

Peculiari-tea

Tanika invited four friends to a tea party, but each guest wanted something different to drink! Break the code on each cup to see what kind of drinks Tanika made for her guests.

Go See Santa

There are certainly a lot of people waiting to see Santa. Can you spy where each of these small parts is located in the big picture? The parts might be turned sideways or upside-down!

1.
2.
3.
4.
5.
6.

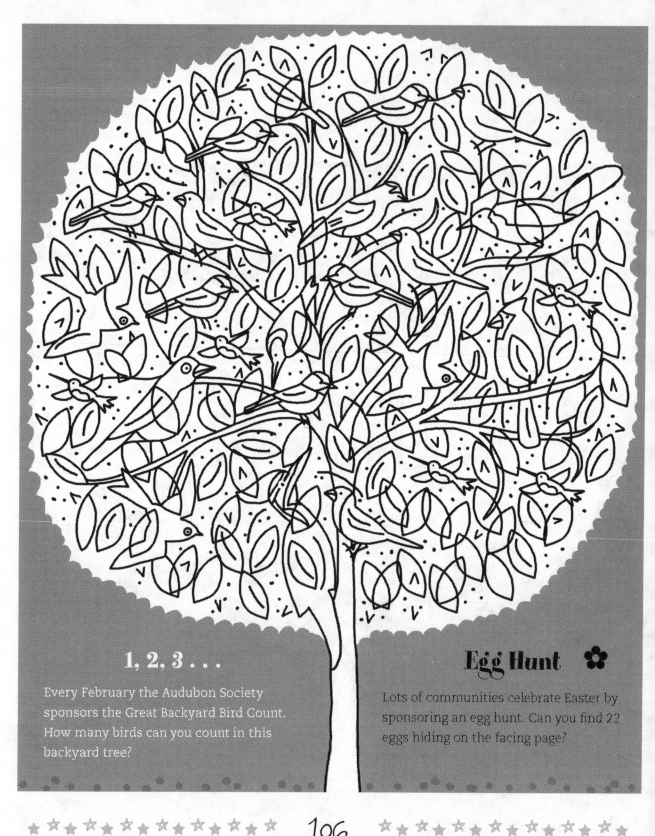

1, 2, 3 . . .

Every February the Audubon Society sponsors the Great Backyard Bird Count. How many birds can you count in this backyard tree?

Egg Hunt ❀

Lots of communities celebrate Easter by sponsoring an egg hunt. Can you find 22 eggs hiding on the facing page?

Crazy Costume

Chloe is having a hard time deciding what to wear to Zoe's costume party. Use the clues to figure out what Chloe finally decided to wear. Circle her choices.

HINT: The party has an "ocean" theme!

She did not wear boots or clogs.

She did wear a dress, but it did not have polka dots.

She did wear something on her head, but it wasn't a hat.

She did wear something around her neck, but it wasn't a scarf.

She did carry something, but it wasn't an umbrella.

Sorting the Loot

You've dumped out your trick-or-treat bag. Now see if you can answer the following questions:

* How many different kinds of treats are there?
* Of which treat is there only one?
* Which treat was given the most?

* How much do the coins add up to?
* Which is your favorite treat?
* Are there more spider rings or swirly mints?

Monika's Menorah

Can you find the one menorah that matches Monika's list?

The menorah to look for has...

...room for 8 candles
(plus the shamas)
...a Star of David
...branches that curve
...a dark base

Festive 4th of July

The 4th of July is when we honor the birthday of the United States. Many small towns have a celebration where everyone joins in! Can you find the 13 stars hiding in this town's parade?

April Fool!

April 1st is a day for practical jokes and silly hoax! See if you can find the 12 things that are not as they should be, and the 1 thing that seems like it could be true but really isn't!

APPENDIX

Online Fun

If you have finished this book and want to do more hidden picture puzzles, here are a few websites you will find very interesting! Some of them are animated, so the pictures dance or move while you try to find them.

BrainBashers
www.brainbashers.com
This site has thousands of brain teasers, puzzles, riddles, games, and optical illusions. There are several daily puzzles, ranging from easy to challenging.

Cool Optical Illusions
www.coolopticalillusions.com
This site is loaded with more than 140 different optic tricks and illusions. Some explain how the illusion works, and many can be printed so you can show your friends.

Fun Brain
www.funbrain.com
This is an education site for K–8 kids and teachers. Search for games by topic—such as art, geography, history, language, technology—or by grade level.

Highlights Kids
www.highlightskids.com
The Highlights for Children website has many free picture puzzles available, with no registration required. Each hidden picture puzzle has three levels of difficulty, so they are challenging for all ages!

JigZone
www.jigzone.com
JigZone is the perfect online site for jigsaw puzzle lovers. Just pick a picture and the number of pieces you prefer. Then click the mouse and drag the pieces to their proper place. You can even upload your own photos and turn them into puzzles!

Kids-Puzzles
www.kids-puzzles.com
These hidden picture puzzles look like ordinary black and white drawings. But when you click on a hidden object, it pops into full color and moves across the page to take its place in the list of objects you are looking for! This site also has a section of hidden picture problems, connect-the-dot puzzles, matching games, word search puzzles, and mazes.

Kidwizard
www.kidwizard.com

This award-winning, fun, and educational site for kids 6–12 years old has a magical slant that focuses on dragons, unicorns, knights, fairies, and the like. Includes mazes, quizzes, logic puzzles, crosswords, word searches, dot-to-dots, and various other types of puzzles.

National Geographic Kids
www.nationalgeographic.com/ngkids

Here you'll find all kinds of wild and wacky games, brain teasers, quizzes, and picture puzzles. Includes a game archive full of challenging activities.

National Institute of Environmental Health Sciences Kids' Pages
www.niehs.nih.gov/kids

This fun site was prepared by the National Institute of Environmental Health Sciences. From the home page, click on the link for Fun and Games. After you have found all the objects in each picture, you can color the picture online, too! Explore additional links for Games and Puzzles, Coloring, Songs, Jokes, Illusions, and Riddles and Brainteasers.

Puzzle Choice
www.puzzlechoice.com

This family-friendly site has a "kid's choice" section. It includes crosswords, word searches, picture puzzles, logic puzzles, and more.

Wimzie's Website
www.wimzie.com

Once you get to the homepage, follow the links from Kids to Wimzie Activities. Based on characters from the popular kids TV puppet show "Wimzie's House," these puzzles are designed for younger kids.

PUZZLE SOLUTIONS

page 6 ★ Jump Rope

page 8 ★ Jumble of Jacks

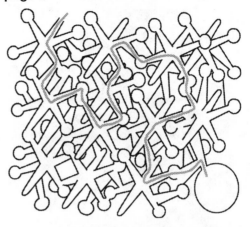

page 7 ★ Pass It On

What should you do if a teacher rolls his eyes at you? Pick them up and roll them back!

page 8 ★ Two of a Kind

page 8 ★ How Many Marbles?

Sandy = 8

Peter = 10

Flo = 12

page 9 ★ Go Fish

PUZZLE SOLUTIONS

page 10 ★ Our Club

page 12 ★ Crazy Hats

page 11 ★ Sleepover

page 13 ★ Driveway Art

PUZZLE SOLUTIONS

page 14 ★ Goal!

page 16 ★ In the Shadows

page 15 ★ Choo Choo

page 18 ★ Peacock

PAIR OF PANTS, PANSY, PAPERCLIP, PARACHUTE, PATCH, PAW PRINT, PEANUT, PEAR, PENGUIN, PENNY, PIECE OF PIE, PIG, PIN, POSTAGE STAMP, POT, PURSE, PUSHPIN

PUZZLE SOLUTIONS

page 19 ★ **Bird Watching**

page 20 ★ **Leaping Lizards**

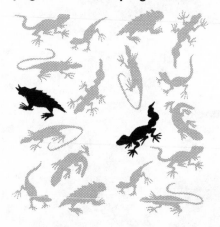

page 21 ★ **Pig Pen**

page 21 ★ **Trick Question 1**

16-5-5 5-25-5 7-5-5

PEE EYE GEE

page 21 ★ **Trick Question 2**

Farmer Jane has only two pigs—one of them is brown, and one of them is pink!

page 22 ★ **Rescue Dogs**

page 23 ★ **Beep Beep**

PUZZLE SOLUTIONS

page 24 ★ **Great Goldfish**

page 26 ★ **What Pet Did Annie Get?**

page 28 ★ **Best Friends**

page 25 ★ **Panda?**

It is easier to find the shy panda if you turn the puzzle page upside-down!

page 30 ★ **In the Wild**

1. Spoon instead of shovel
2. Umbrella instead of pot
3. Eyeglasses instead of wood
4. Birthday candle instead of log
5. Thimble instead of bucket
6. Dice instead of stool
7. Pencil instead of fishing pole
8. Clock instead of fishing bobber
9. Pea pod instead of canoe
10. Easter basket instead of picnic basket
11. Swirly candy instead of bed roll
12. Coffee cup instead of tent
13. Playing card instead of beach towel
14. Christmas stocking instead of socks

PUZZLE SOLUTIONS

page 30 ★ **Triangle Teaser**

page 31 ★ **Court Count**

page 32 ★ **ZAP!**

There are 11 ZAPs on this page. Multiply that by 10 for a score of 110. Congratulations, you win!

page 33 ★ **Sticky Stamps**

1. There are five bird stamps and only four patriotic stamps.

2. Birds are on the most number of stamps.

3. Teddy bears are on the four almost-identical stamps.

4. The stamp with the fox on it has the most postage (48 cents).

page 34 ★ **Downhill Race**

page 35 ★ **Fractured Football**

PUZZLE SOLUTIONS

page 35 ★ **Uniform Uniforms**

page 37 ★ **Perfect Play**

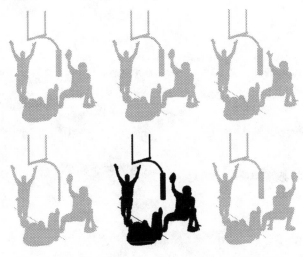

page 36 ★ **College Copies**

page 38 ★ **Build a Model**

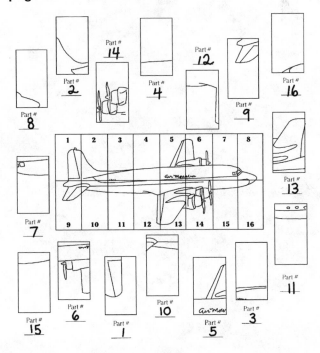

PUZZLE SOLUTIONS

page 39 ★ **X-treme Sports**

BUNGEE JUMPING

ROCK CLIMBING

SKY DIVING

MOTORCYCLE RACING

page 39 ★ **On Your Mark!**

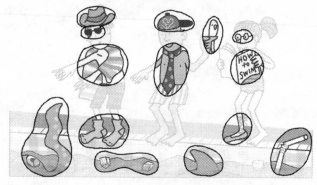

page 40 ★ **Goofy Golf**

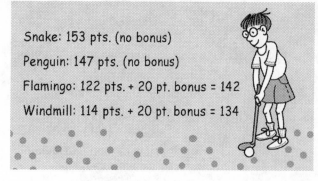

Snake: 153 pts. (no bonus)

Penguin: 147 pts. (no bonus)

Flamingo: 122 pts. + 20 pt. bonus = 142

Windmill: 114 pts. + 20 pt. bonus = 134

page 42 ★ **Name Game**

page 43 ★ **Who's in the Family?**

There are five people and three pets in this family: Dad, Mom, Grandmother, school-age child, baby, dog, cat, goldfish. Hints: Look at the pairs of shoes, the coats and hats, the mugs and card on the table, the balloons, the pet dishes, and the poster on the fridge.

page 44 ★ **Sorting Laundry**

1. There are 12 long socks, which make 6 perfect pairs. There are only 11 short socks, which makes 5 pairs plus 1 extra.

2. Only one pair of long socks has three stripes at the top.

3. There are more shorts (8) than T-shirts (7).

4. No. Shirt number 4 is missing.

PUZZLE SOLUTIONS

page 45 ★ **Good Night!**

page 47 ★ **Twice the Fun**

page 46 ★ **What's Weird?**

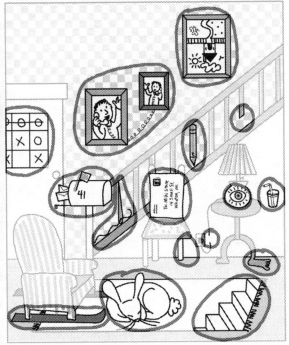

page 48 ★ **Yard Work**

PUZZLE SOLUTIONS

page 49 ★ Family Reunion

page 50 ★ Stephanie's Sleepover

page 50 ★ Nice Neighbors

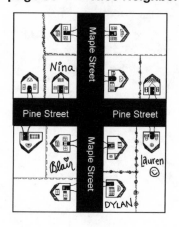

page 51 ★ Family Portrait

page 52 ★ Dish Duty

PUZZLE SOLUTIONS

page 54 ★ **At the Shore**

6 crabs   **10** scallops   **7** jellyfish   **8** starfish

page 56 ★ **Walrus**

page 55 ★ **Sharks, Etc.**

There are 24 sharks and 7 jellyfish. The sock is the item that doesn't belong!

page 57 ★ **Where Are We?**

Answer: Lost! No penguins live in the arctic.
Most of them live in Antarctica!

PUZZLE SOLUTIONS

page 58 ★ **A Day at the Beach**

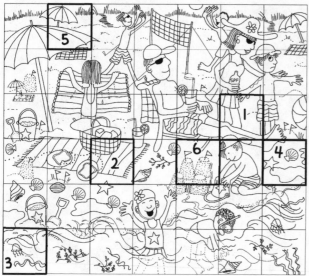

page 60 ★ **Shell Talk**

There is a lot to see under the sea!

pages 60-61 ★ **School of Fish**

There are 82 fish in the school that stretches across both pages. Actually, there are 83 if you add the one little fish which is scared of the submarine!

page 59 ★ **Lights, Please!**

pages 60-61 ★ **ABC and What's Dot?**

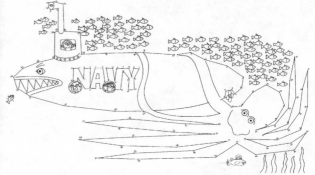

Both a submarine and an octopus travel under the sea.

PUZZLE SOLUTIONS

page 62 ★ **X Marks the Spot**

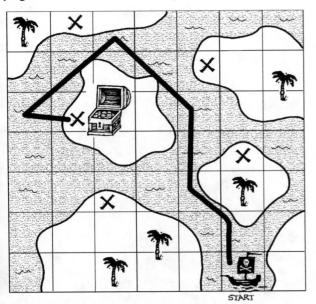

page 63 ★ **Crusty Fellow**

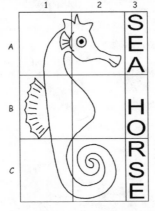

Answer: He was too shellfish (selfish)!

page 63 ★ **Create a Fish**

Here are some sample "silly fish." Your drawings will probably look very different from these!

1.  TRUMPETFISH

2. CLOWNFISH

3.  FLAGTAIL

page 64 ★ **Nice Neigh-bor**

page 66 ★ **Just One Bite—Please?**

PUZZLE SOLUTIONS

page 67 ★ S-L-L-L-L-U-U-U-U-R-R-R-P!

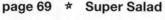

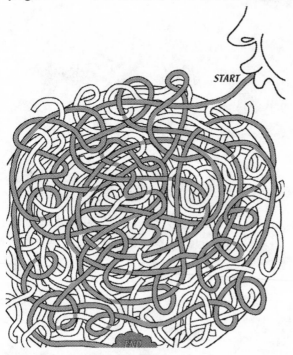

page 69 ★ Super Salad

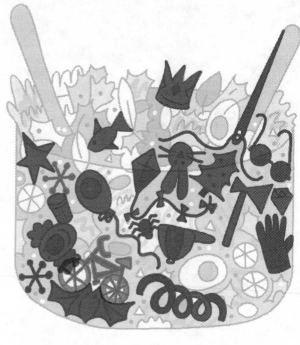

page 68 ★ Sunday Dinner

page 70 ★ Food Fun

★ ★ ★ ★ ★ ★ ★ ★ ★ ★ ★ ★ ★ ★ 130 ★ ★ ★ ★ ★ ★ ★ ★ ★ ★ ★ ★ ★ ★

PUZZLE SOLUTIONS

page 71 ★ Splash!

page 73 ★ Hiding Hot Dogs

page 72 ★ Scoops

page 74 ★ Bunny Salad

PUZZLE SOLUTIONS

page 75 ★ **Fill 'er Up!**

page 78 ★ **Pack Your Bags!**

Things that are the SAME: Cage on the ski pole is the same as the beach ball; ski hat is the same as sleeve of Hawaiian shirt; sole of ski boot is the same as sandal; Ski Snow Mountain brochure is same shape as kite; sun on Ski Sun Mtn. brochure same as sun on bathing suit; mitten same as pattern on kite; snowflake on SKI brochure same as snowflake on sweater; pattern on skis same as pattern on palm tree; daisy on T-shirt same as daisy on sun hat.

Things that are OPPOSITE: The girl in the top picture is wearing a T-shirt, but is packing to go on a cold and snowy vacation, while the other girl is wearing a turtleneck sweater, but is packing for a warm and sunny vacation. The first girl is going to learn to ski on snow, while the girl in the lower right is going to learn how to water ski!

page 75 ★ **Crazy Cookies**

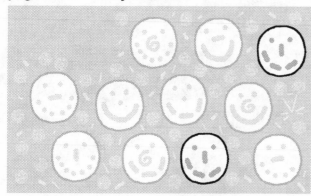

page 79 ★ **Cross-Country Trip**

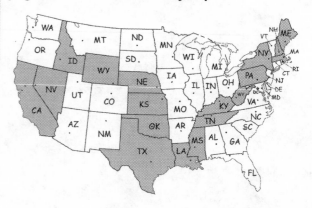

page 76 ★ **Sneaking Treats**

PUZZLE SOLUTIONS

page 80 ★ India

page 82 ★ Mexico

page 81 ★ Peculiar Passport

New Zealand
England
Mexico
Thailand
United States
Norway
North Korea
China
Yugoslavia
Australia

In 2003, the country of Yugoslavia was renamed Serbia and Montenegro. This happened after Yugoslavia's 10-year civil war.

page 83 ★ Road Trip

PUZZLE SOLUTIONS

page 84 ★ **Hidden Jungle**

page 85 ★ **Wish You Were Here**

page 86 ★ **France**

page 87 ★ **Check It Out!**

This family is visiting the state of Missouri. Missouri is known as the "Show Me State" (slogan on the boy's T-shirt). "The Gateway Arch" (Dad's T-shirt) is located in the city of St. Louis, and is the tallest monument in the US. The "world's first ice cream cone" (sign) was said to be sold at the St. Louis World's Fair in 1904. Famous author "Mark Twain" (girl's T-shirt), author of *Tom Sawyer* and *The Adventures of Huckleberry Finn*, was born in Hannibal, MO. "Paddlewheelers" (gift bag) are a famous type of river boat that once traveled up and down the rivers of Missouri transporting goods, passengers, and entertainment.

PUZZLE SOLUTIONS

page 88 ★ The Great Race

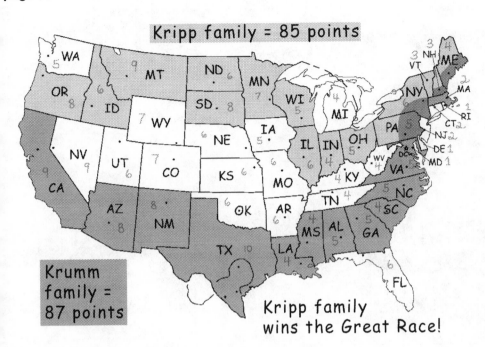

Kripp family = 85 points

Krumm family = 87 points

Kripp family wins the Great Race!

page 90 ★ Ants

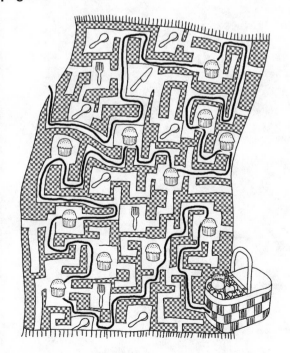

PUZZLE SOLUTIONS

page 91 ★ Creepy Crawlies

page 92 ★ Small But Deadly

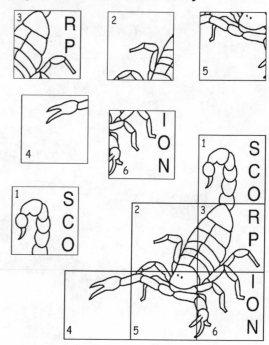

page 92 ★ Small Survivors

S̶ O I T L T S̶
C P̶ E U E̶ T S
B E C D̶ S E T
L E R C K̶ R̶ E
T R I̶ M I E S

1. SPIDERS
2. CRICKET
3. BEETLES
4. LOCUSTS
5. TERMITE

page 93 ★ Summer Nights

PUZZLE SOLUTIONS

page 94 ★ **Why does everyone . . .**

THEY ARE GREAT
AT CATCHING FLIES!

page 96 ★ **Monarch Butterfly**

AMAZING

page 95 ★ **Ssssnakes**

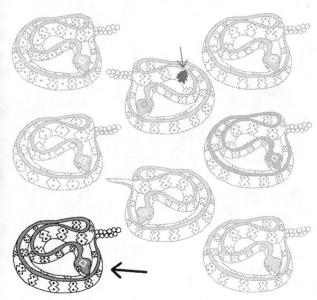

page 97 ★ **Spider's Choice**

French flies!

page 97 ★ **Creaking Stairs**

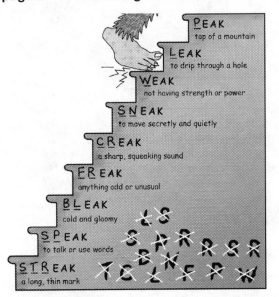

PEAK
top of a mountain

LEAK
to drip through a hole

WEAK
not having strength or power

SNEAK
to move secretly and quietly

CREAK
a sharp, squeaking sound

FREAK
anything odd or unusual

BLEAK
cold and gloomy

SPEAK
to talk or use words

STREAK
a long, thin mark

PUZZLE SOLUTIONS

page 98 ★ **A Bundle of Bugs**

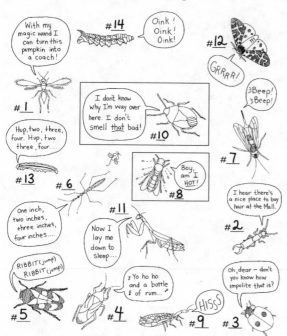

page 99 ★ **Pack Rat**

page 100 ★ **Breezy Butterflies**

PUZZLE SOLUTIONS

page 100 ★ **Batty for Fruit**

1. F I G
2. M A N G O
3. B A N A N A

page 103 ★ **And Many More . . .**

Gramps is 89!

happy birthday

page 102 ★ **Valentine's Day**

BE MINE

page 104 ★ **Happy Half**

HAPPY BIRTHDAY

PUZZLE SOLUTIONS

page 104 ★ **Peculiari-tea**

MILK SHAKE

SODA (Code: A=1, B=2, C=3, etc.)

JUICE (Code: Substitute the letter before each letter of the message.)

ICED TEA

page 106 ★ **1, 2, 3 . . .**

page 105 ★ **Go See Santa**

page 107 ★ **Egg Hunt**

✦ ✦ ✦ ✦ ✦ ✦ ✦ ✦ ✦ ✦ ✦ 140 ✦ ✦ ✦ ✦ ✦ ✦ ✦ ✦ ✦ ✦ ✦

PUZZLE SOLUTIONS

page 108 ★ **Crazy Costume**

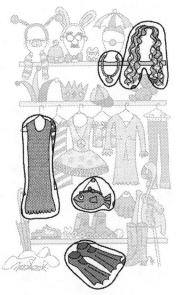

Chloe decided to go as a mermaid!

page 109 ★ **Sorting the Loot**

- HOW MANY DIFFERENT KINDS OF TREATS ARE THERE? There are 12 different kinds: gum, sticker, chocolate "choco" bar, lollipop, YUM YUM YUM candy, coin, candy corn (each bagful counts as one), swirly mint, spider ring, chocolate chip cookie, Bitz candy, fireball.

- OF WHICH TREAT IS THERE ONLY ONE? There is only one fireball.

- WHICH TREAT WAS GIVEN THE MOST? Lollipops (there are 11), though chocolate is a close second with 10 pieces.

- HOW MUCH DO THE COINS ADD UP TO? $2.50

- WHICH IS YOUR FAVORITE TREAT? Everyone will have a different favorite!

- ARE THERE MORE SPIDER RINGS OR SWIRLY MINTS? There are the same number (8).

page 110 ★ **Monika's Menorah**

PUZZLE SOLUTIONS

page 111 ★ **Festive 4th of July**

page 112 ★ **April Fool!**

The story about Swiss spaghetti farmers was aired on the British news on April 1, 1957. Hundreds of people called the tv station to find out how they cold grow their own spaghetti trees!